The Day I Discovered a Dinosaur Bone?!

Adventures of the Barnyard Boys

Melanie Larson

Illustrator: Rahul Ghosh

M Larson Books

Saskatchewan, Canada

M Larson Books

Copyright M Larson

ISBN 978-1-9992683-0-5

June 2021

All rights reserved.

No part of this publication may be reproduced or stored in a retrieval system, or transmitted in any form or by any means, electronic, mechanical, recording, or otherwise, without written permission of the publisher, M Larson Books, Saskatchewan, Canada. In the case of photocopying, a licence must be obtained from Access Copyright (Canadian Copyright Licensing Agency), 56 Wellesley Street West, Suite 320, Toronto, Ontario M5S 2S3 (1-800-893-5777) or visit www.accesscopyright.ca.

Acknowledgements

Special thank you to Paleontologist Hallie P. Street, Ph.D., for her valuable contributions and feedback in the creation of this book.

About the Author

Melanie Larson is a lucky Mom of three and farm wife in rural Saskatchewan. Besides creating children's books, Melanie works as an Environmental Consultant in western Canada. Her other books include *Count Them! 50 Tractor Troubles*, *The Alphabet Construction Troubles*, *The Colours in Tractor Troubles* and *The Day I Lost My Bear in Cypress Hills*. Melanie and her family stay busy by raising Kunekune pigs, playing sports and looking for dinosaur bones in Saskatchewan.

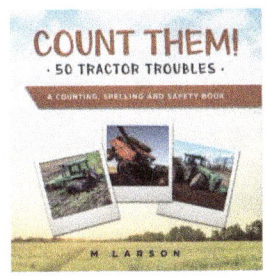  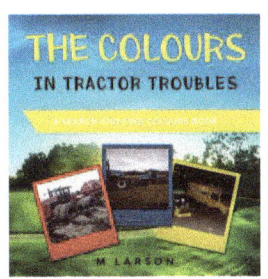 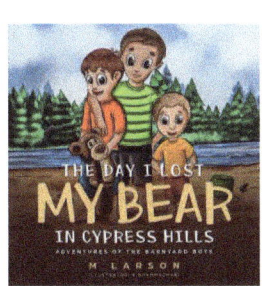

www.mlarsonbooks.com

Hi! My name is Finn, and I am 6 years old. I love dinosaurs, and so does my older brother Owen and my little brother Dez. We are watching our favorite dinosaur movie. Did you know that the world's largest *Tyrannosaurus rex* fossil was discovered right here in Saskatchewan?

Fun fact: The largest *Tyrannosaurus rex* fossil ever found throughout the world was discovered near Eastend, Saskatchewan by Robert Gebhardt, a high school principal, in 1991. The fossil's nickname is "Scotty."

After our movie ended, Owen thought we should search for some dinosaur bones, too! We love going on new adventures! We will need shovels, brushes, chisels and whatever Dez decided to use!

First, we headed to the sandbox to look for dinosaur bones. I bet we have a short-necked plesiosaur right in our own backyard! We dug a deep hole, and Owen found something! Unfortunately, Mom said, "That's just an old, broken toy truck." Maybe we will have better luck finding a dinosaur bone at the beach?!

Fun fact: A short-necked plesiosaur *(Dolichorhynchops herschelensis)* is the only one of its kind ever found throughout the world. The skeleton was discovered near Herschel, Saskatchewan in 1990.

The beach was a lot of fun! We swam in the water and played in the sand. We did not forget why we came, though, and got to work. It wasn't long before I found something hiding in the sand. Once again, Mom said, "That's not a dinosaur bone." It was just a heavy piece of driftwood. Maybe we need to look somewhere else.

Back at home, we sat in the kitchen while Dad cleaned up after dinner. "Dad! They are breaking a dinosaur bone!" Dez exclaimed. "No, that's a chicken bone from dinner, Dez!" Dad said, shaking his head. "A dinosaur bone would be much larger, heavier and harder to break." Owen, Dez and I had pretty much given up on finding a dinosaur bone.

Fun fact: While birds, like chickens, might not look like their extinct relatives, they share ancestral paths and DNA with dinosaurs.

The next day, we went to Grandma and Grandpa's ranch to help them with some odd jobs and look for more dinosaur bones, of course! Owen and Dez learned about the extinction boundary while horseback riding with Grandpa. I helped Grandma plant her flowerbeds. My job was to dig a lot of little holes, and Grandma would plant one orange lily in each hole. Suddenly, my little shovel hit something in the ground! I excitedly dug it out. Maybe I finally found a dinosaur bone!

Fun fact: The hillsides in Saskatchewan have excellent examples of the "extinction boundary," or the exact layers of rock that mark the extinction of the dinosaurs and the end of the Cretaceous Period.

We dug out our new discovery from the ground. It was long and very heavy! I hoped it was a bone from a *Thescelosaurus assiniboiensis*, but we couldn't tell for sure! So, we decided to take it to a dinosaur museum to learn more from an expert. The "bone" was so big that it would not fit inside our van! Dad had to safety strap it to the roof!

Fun fact: The small, plant-eating dinosaur, *Thescelosaurus assiniboiensis*, was about the size of a deer. This dinosaur was also bipedal, meaning it used only its two back legs to move around. These small dinosaur fossils have only been found in Saskatchewan.

On the way to the museum, we looked at dinosaur books to see if we could figure out what I had found in Grandma's flowerbed. Owen said, "Maybe it's a *Megacerops*!" I said, "Maybe it's an *Edmontosaurus*." And Dez said, "Maybe it's a tractor!"

Fun fact: There are two main dinosaur museums in Saskatchewan. The T.rex Discovery Centre is in Eastend, SK and features hands-on learning activities for both children and adults. The Royal Saskatchewan Museum is in Regina, SK. This museum teaches visitors about Saskatchewan's natural history and aboriginal cultures, past and present. Both museums have a life-size model of the world's largest *Tyrannosaurus rex*, Scotty, on display.

It was a long drive to the museum, so we started thinking about what life would be like if dinosaurs still roamed the Earth. "Can you imagine a plesiosaur in the pool?" I asked my family.

Fun fact: In 1992, "Mo," the Ponteix Plesiosaur, was found 6 kilometres northeast of Ponteix, SK. Mo was a sea reptile that lived about 70 million years ago and reached a length of more than 11 meters.

Owen said, "We probably wouldn't be able to go downtown anymore if there were *Tyrannosaurus rex* walking around everywhere! We wouldn't even be able to go to a restaurant!"

We finally arrived at the dinosaur museum. We saw dinosaur bones belonging to *Triceratops*, *Mosasaurus*, *Troodon* and *Ankylosaurus*. We also saw ancient crocodile bones, too! There were so many neat animals that once roamed the same land we live on today, but there are none living now. They are extinct! We also learned about coprolite which is the official word for dinosaur poop!

Fun fact: In 1991, scientists from the Royal Saskatchewan Museum and the Canadian Museum of Nature discovered a 6-metre-long fossil of an ancient crocodile on the banks of the Carrot River. The scientists named the *Terminonaris robustus* specimen "Big Bert." "Big Bert" is very well preserved and the only one of its kind found in Canada.

We met with a dinosaur expert called a paleontologist. As paleontologist George examined the piece I found in Grandma's flowerbed, we excitedly waited to learn what I actually dug up. Finally, he told us that I didn't discover a dinosaur bone after all. I found something called "petrified wood." This special type of fossil was once a tree! After the tree fell down a long time ago, it was covered by soil and water. Eventually, the wood was replaced by minerals found in the Earth's soil. George said this piece of petrified wood could be more than 65 million years old! "It's as old as Grandpa!" I exclaimed.

Fun fact: Fossils are the remains of living things that existed more than 10,000 years ago. In 1874, the first dinosaur fossil was found in Grasslands National Park in Canada. George Dawson, a pioneer geologist, found the bones of a *hadrosaur*, a "duck billed" dinosaur, in the Killdeer Badlands.

Back at home, we went right back to work! George told us that there could be even more petrified wood in our very own neighborhood. Even Mom and Dad are helping us search the yard! I hope we find some more fossils soon!

Fun fact: Plant and small animal fossils also help paleontologists understand what the world looked and felt like when the dinosaurs lived on Earth. The kinds of plant fossils found in southern Saskatchewan tell scientists that Saskatchewan was much warmer and wetter than it is today.

Can you find these animals hiding somewhere in this book?

Dinosaurs were our ancestors:

We evolved after dinosaurs went extinct:

Our ancestors evolved before dinosaurs:

We evolved alongside dinosaurs:

www.ingramcontent.com/pod-product-compliance
Lightning Source LLC
Chambersburg PA
CBHW061107070526
44579CB00011B/164